I0797908

Caitlin Clark
Anton Vega
B1G
IOWA
22
NCAA
OFFICIAL GAME BALL
Wilson
EVO NXT
childsworld.com

The Child's World
childsworld.com

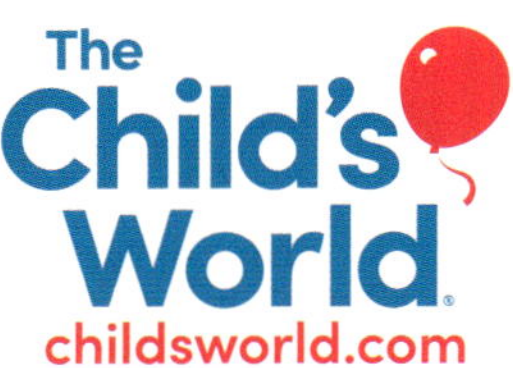

Published by The Child's World®
800-599-READ • www.childsworld.com

Photography Credits
Photographs ©: Nick Wass/AP Images, cover, 1; Shutterstock Images, 5, 7, 27; Jacob Boomsma/Shutterstock Images, 9; Nicola Patterson/Shutterstock Images, 10; Carmen Mandato/Getty Images Sport/Getty Images, 13; Aaron J. Thornton/Getty Images Sport/Getty Images, 15; Bailey Hillesheim/Icon Sportswire, 17; Steph Chambers/Getty Images Sport/Getty Images, 19; Matthew Holst/Getty Images Sport/Getty Images, 21; Sam Wagner/Shutterstock Images, 23; State Farm, 24; Joseph Hendrickson/Shutterstock Images, 28; Maddie Meyer/Getty Images Sport/Getty Images, 29; Design elements from Shutterstock Images

ISBN Information
9781503875760 (Reinforced Library Binding)
9781503876668 (Portable Document Format)
9781503877160 (Online Multi-user eBook)
9781503877788 (Electronic Publication)

LCCN 2025938126

Printed in the United States of America

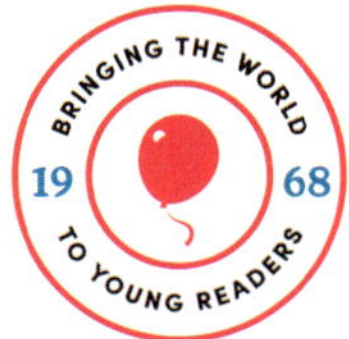

ABOUT THE AUTHOR
Anton Vega is a sportswriter and author from El Paso, Texas. He grew up playing basketball and watches many NBA, WNBA, and college basketball games.

TABLE of CONTENTS

CHAPTER ONE

Rookie Sensation

Indiana Fever guard Caitlin Clark dribbled hard to her right. Then she stopped in an instant. She stepped back to create space from her defender. With room to shoot, Clark drained a deep three-pointer.

It was September 4, 2024. Clark's Indiana Fever were facing the Los Angeles Sparks. Clark had been lighting up the Women's National Basketball Association (WNBA) during her **rookie** year. And her play had helped the Fever climb the standings. Before this game, the Fever had clinched a spot in the playoffs. It was their first time in 8 years! Now, more than 16,000 fans filled Indiana's arena to watch one of the league's brightest stars.

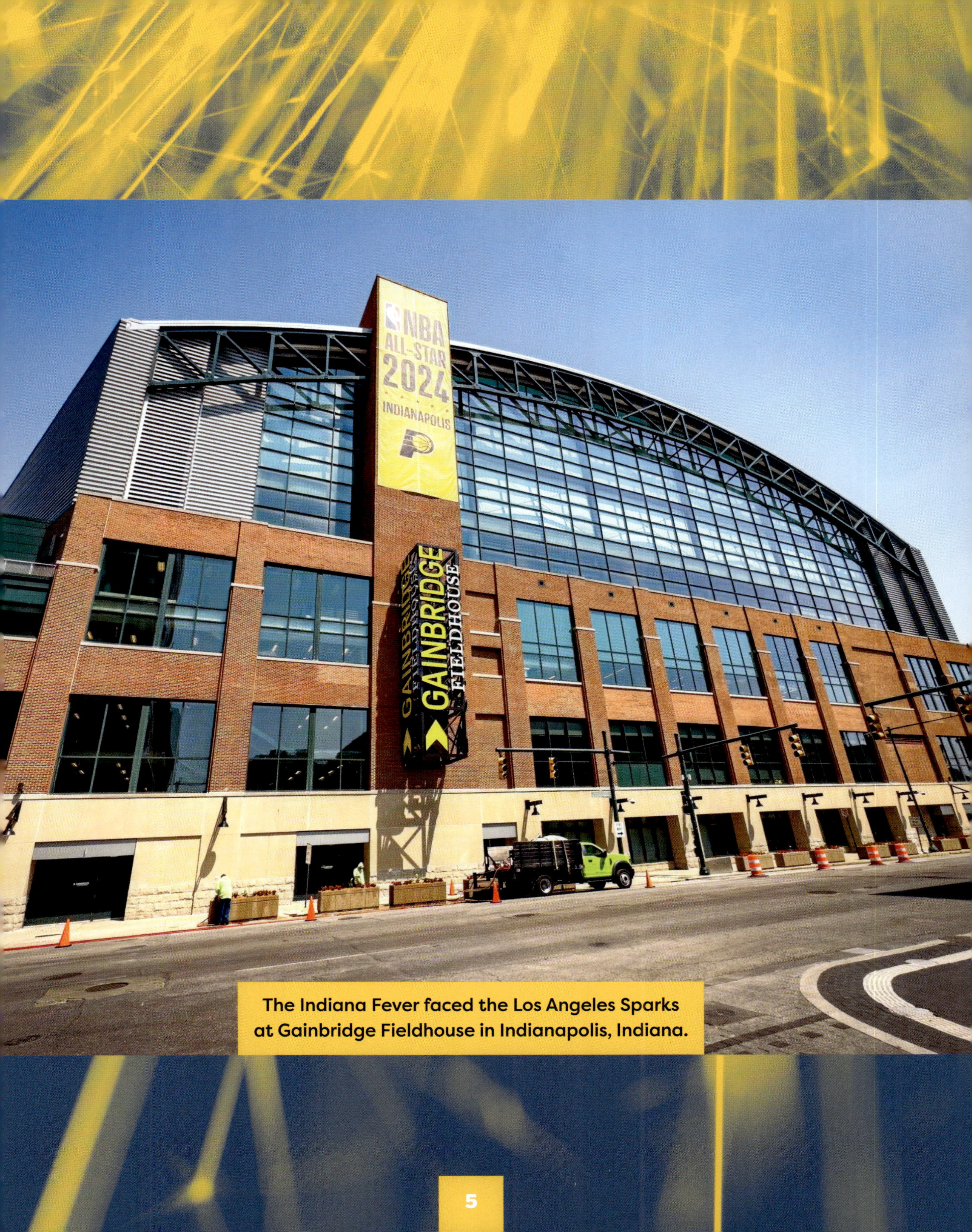

The Indiana Fever faced the Los Angeles Sparks at Gainbridge Fieldhouse in Indianapolis, Indiana.

Clark's three-pointer put the Fever up 74–68 early in the fourth quarter. On the next Fever possession, Clark stormed past two defenders on her way to the basket. When a third defender stepped in her way, Clark did not panic. She passed the ball behind her back to teammate NaLyssa Smith. Then Smith scored to extend Indiana's lead. The Fever hung on to win 93–86.

Clark had been making flashy plays throughout her rookie season. Basketball fans could not get enough of her deep jump shots and creative passes. Wherever the Fever played, massive crowds followed. They wanted to watch Clark put on a show.

TRIPLE-DOUBLE MACHINE

Clark finished the game against the Sparks with 24 points, ten rebounds, and ten assists. Those stats gave her a triple-double. Two months earlier, Clark became the first rookie in WNBA history to record a triple-double. She became just the fifth player in league history to have more than one triple-double in a season.

Clark was *Time* magazine's 2024 Athlete of the Year.

During her 4 years at the University of Iowa, Clark shattered scoring records. Her exciting playing style helped bring the popularity of women's basketball to new heights. And her historic college career led to massive expectations for her rookie year in the WNBA. Clark lived up to the hype in the WNBA to become one of its biggest stars. And she was just getting started.

CHAPTER TWO

Hometown Hero

Caitlin Clark was born on January 22, 2002, in Des Moines, Iowa. Caitlin grew up in a competitive household. She often played basketball with her two brothers. No matter what Caitlin did, she wanted to be the best at it.

Caitlin's dad, Brent, played basketball and baseball in college. He encouraged Caitlin to try different sports as a kid. Caitlin played golf, softball, soccer, tennis, and volleyball. But basketball was always her favorite. Caitlin began playing in basketball leagues when she was 5 years old. When Caitlin was in middle school, college coaches started noticing how talented she was.

Des Moines (pictured) is the capital of Iowa. Caitlin grew up near the city.

Caitlin was a star athlete in high school. She eventually decided to go to the University of Iowa.

In 2016, Caitlin made the **varsity** basketball team at Dowling Catholic High School as a freshman. By her junior year, she was one of the best players in the country. That season, Caitlin set a new Iowa high school record with 13 three-pointers in a game. She finished with 60 points. After the season, she was named Iowa's Gatorade Player of the Year. This is an award given to high school student-athletes to recognize their achievements.

Caitlin earned that honor again as a senior after averaging more than 30 points per game. During her senior year, she thought about where she would go to college. Growing up, Caitlin looked up to University of Connecticut (UConn) star Maya Moore. Caitlin thought she would end up playing at UConn someday, too. Most of the top basketball schools in the country **recruited** Caitlin. But UConn was not one of them. So Caitlin decided between Iowa and Notre Dame. She chose to stay close to home and committed to Iowa.

Caitlin dreamed of leading the Hawkeyes to the Final Four. The Final Four is the last stage of March Madness. March Madness is a National Collegiate Athletic Association (NCAA) single-elimination basketball tournament. As teams are eliminated, the best teams battle through the Sweet 16, Elite Eight, and Final Four for a spot in the national championship.

In November 2020, Caitlin played her first game with the Hawkeyes. She showed off her scoring skills and finished the game with 27 points. That performance was a sign of things to come.

IN HER WORDS

Caitlin Clark explained her decision to play for Iowa instead of one of the traditional basketball powerhouses, often called blue bloods. She said:

> **Iowa was really good at women's basketball before I went there, too. . . . I wanted to go somewhere that was good but maybe hadn't been like a blue blood . . . in quite a few years, and kind of help them get back to that. . . . It was obviously my home state, too. Two hours from where I grew up, so the perfect distance.**

Source: Lundberg, Robin. "Caitlin Clark Details Why She Chose Iowa over Notre Dame for College Basketball Home." Women's Fastbreak, *January 2, 2025. www.si.com.*

Caitlin pushes past Connecticut Huskies player Christyn Williams in the 2021 Sweet 16 matchup.

Caitlin led the country with 26.6 points per game as a freshman. In her first NCAA March Madness Tournament, Caitlin led Iowa to wins against Central Michigan and Kentucky. That set up a Sweet 16 matchup against UConn. Caitlin scored 21 points against them. But it was not enough. UConn won 92–72. After the game, legendary UConn coach Geno Auriemma told Caitlin she had a bright future.

Caitlin quickly proved Auriemma correct. As a sophomore, Caitlin recorded the most points and assists per game in the nation. She helped Iowa stack up wins, too. That season, the Hawkeyes tied for the best regular-season record in the Big Ten Conference. They had not done that in 14 years.

Caitlin continued to spark Iowa's offense in the Big Ten Tournament. In a semifinal matchup against Nebraska, Caitlin scored 41 points. This sent Iowa to the championship game. There, Iowa beat Indiana to win the conference tournament title.

INTERNATIONAL SUCCESS

Caitlin Clark played in the Under-19 Basketball World Cup in 2019 and 2021. She helped the United States win gold both times. In 2021, she earned tournament Most Valuable Player (MVP) honors. Caitlin is one of six US players to compete in two U19 World Cups.

Iowa beat Indiana 74–67 in 2022 to win the Big Ten Tournament title. Clark scored 18 points.

Iowa easily won its first game in that year's NCAA Tournament. In the second round, Iowa hosted Creighton. Caitlin had an off game. She missed 15 of her 19 shot attempts. Creighton won 64–62 to **upset** the Hawkeyes and end their season. Caitlin was devastated. But she was determined to come back stronger than ever.

CHAPTER THREE

Rising Star

Caitlin Clark used the loss against Creighton as motivation for her junior year. She worked out in the off-season to get stronger and faster. She also spent hours practicing in the gym each day.

The work paid off for Clark. She increased her average points and assists per game for the third year in a row. And she continued to shine in the Big Ten Tournament. Iowa took on Ohio State in the championship game. Clark put on a show for fans, recording a triple-double of 30 points, 17 assists, and ten rebounds. The Hawkeyes blew out Ohio State 105–72 to defend their Big Ten Tournament title.

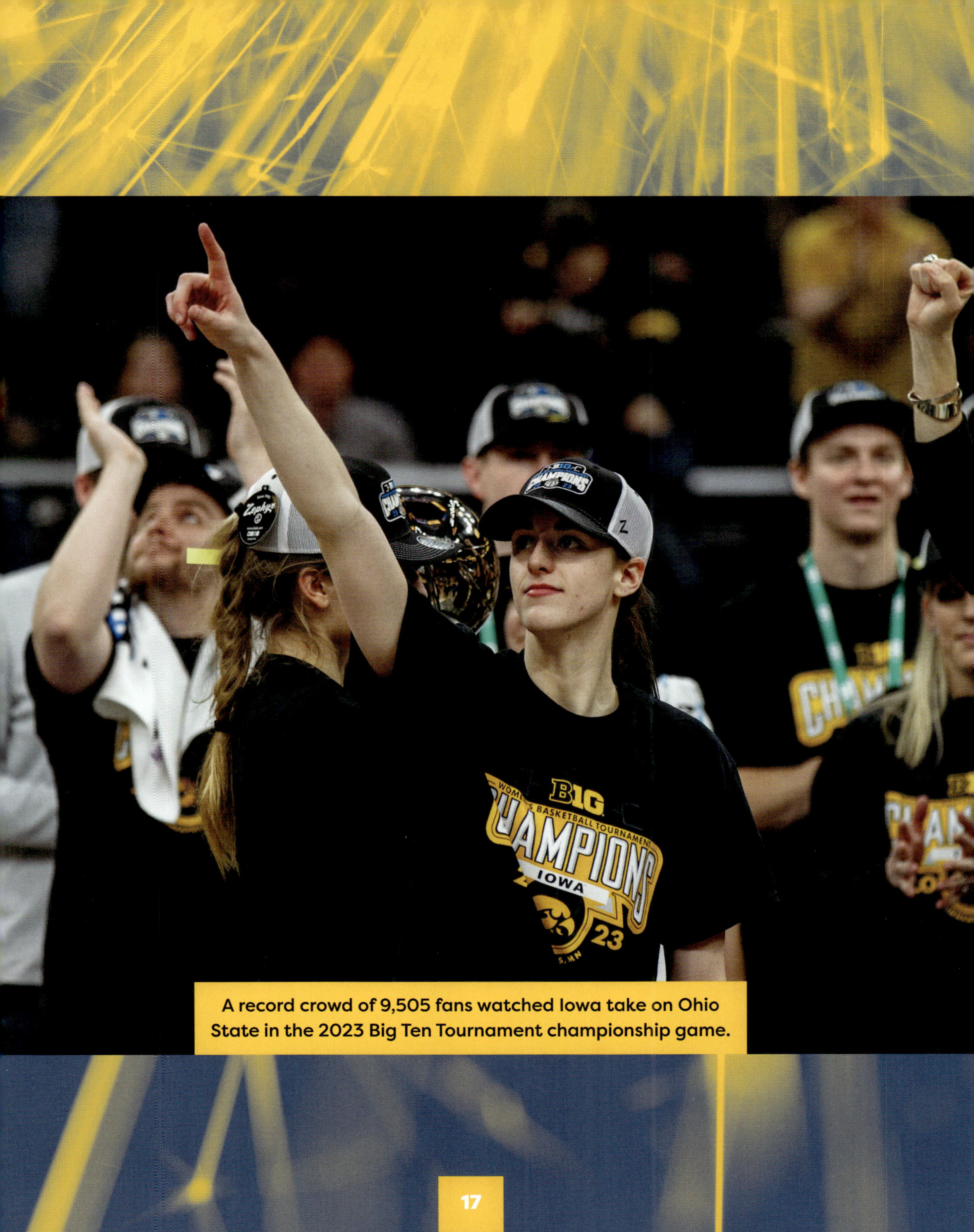

A record crowd of 9,505 fans watched Iowa take on Ohio State in the 2023 Big Ten Tournament championship game.

Clark thought Iowa was good enough to win a national championship. She remained focused on that goal heading into the NCAA Tournament. In the first three games, Clark scored with ease. She set up her teammates to score, too. Iowa won three games to advance to the Elite Eight.

Louisville could not slow Clark down in the Elite Eight. Clark hit eight three-pointers. She finished the game with 41 points and another triple-double. Once the final buzzer sounded, Clark and her teammates ran onto the court to celebrate. For the first time in 30 years, Iowa was headed to the Final Four!

Clark had dreamed of this moment for years. Now the Hawkeyes faced a nightmare matchup. South Carolina was the defending champion. The Gamecocks rolled into the Final Four with a perfect 36–0 record.

Clark was not fazed, though. With under 8 minutes left in the game, Iowa led 64–62. Clark pulled up for a jump shot from way beyond the three-point line. The ball swished home to put the Hawkeyes up by five. Clark scored all of Iowa's points from there to finish with 41 points. Her scoring outburst led the Hawkeyes to their first national championship game.

Clark defends against Mykasa Robinson in Iowa's game against Louisville.

Star forward Angel Reese and Louisiana State University (LSU) awaited Iowa in the title game. In the biggest game of her life, Clark delivered. She made eight three-pointers and scored 30 points. But Iowa could not slow down LSU's offense. The Tigers beat Iowa 102–85 to win the championship.

A record 9.9 million viewers tuned in for the championship game. And the excitement for Clark only grew during her senior year. Every home and away game Iowa played that season sold out. Some fans paid hundreds of dollars for the chance to see Clark play.

Whatever the price, fans got their money's worth. Clark went on a scoring tear as a senior. Near the end of the regular season, Clark was close to becoming the all-time leading scorer in NCAA women's basketball history. When Iowa hosted Michigan on February 15, 2024, Clark needed eight points to break the record.

Clark scored five points in the opening 42 seconds. A couple minutes later, Clark received a pass behind half-court. Clark took two dribbles forward then buried a deep three-pointer. Iowa's home fans erupted in cheers to celebrate their star's historic moment.

ALL OVER TV

After Clark's freshman year, the NCAA began allowing athletes to make money off their name, image, and likeness. Soon, Clark appeared in dozens of commercials. State Farm, Gatorade, and Nike were just some of the brands that aired ads starring Clark.

Clark celebrates after beating the NCAA women's all-time scoring record.

Clark was not done setting records. About 2 weeks later, Clark scored her 3,668th career point. That broke LSU legend Pete Maravich's 54-year-old record for most points in college basketball history. With no record left to chase, Clark's final goal was to lift Iowa to a national championship.

CHAPTER FOUR

Going Pro

Two weeks before the 2024 Big Ten Tournament began, every game sold out. Facing Nebraska in the championship game, Clark made a late **layup** to send the game to **overtime**. Then, she drained a three-pointer late in the extra period to give Iowa a lead. The Hawkeyes held on to win their third straight Big Ten Tournament championship.

In the NCAA Tournament, Clark led Iowa back to the Elite Eight. A highly anticipated rematch against Angel Reese and LSU awaited. During the game's first possession, Clark buried a three-pointer. She would go on to make eight more throughout the game. Clark scored 41 points and brought Iowa back into the Final Four.

Iowa faced Nebraska in the 2024 Big Ten Tournament at Target Center in Minneapolis, Minnesota.

Clark was the first college athlete to star in a State Farm commercial.

Clark helped Iowa beat UConn in the semifinals. The Hawkeyes then faced an undefeated South Carolina for the championship. In her final college game, Clark started out hot. She lit up the Gamecocks for 18 points in the first quarter. No player had ever scored that many points in a quarter of a championship game. But South Carolina battled back. Despite 30 points from Clark, the Gamecocks finished a perfect season with an 87–75 win.

While the loss was disappointing for Clark, she had once again lifted the popularity of women's basketball. Starting with the Elite Eight, the last three games of Clark's Iowa career were the most-watched women's college basketball games ever. A record 18.7 million viewers watched the championship game.

Only a week after her college career ended, Clark traveled to New York City for the WNBA **Draft**. Millions of fans tuned in to see the Indiana Fever select Clark with the top pick. People looked forward to what Clark would do in the WNBA.

Clark had adjusted to the college game right away. But adapting to the WNBA took some time. The Fever faced the Connecticut Sun in Clark's first game. The Sun had the league's best defense in 2023, and they hounded Clark. Connecticut forced Clark to commit ten turnovers, leading to a 92–71 win for the Sun.

The Fever lost their first five games of the season. By their ninth game, they had only one win. Indiana had been one of the worst teams in the WNBA for almost a decade. Even with a new star, the Fever seemed destined for another losing season.

Clark improved as the season went on. She often showed off her elite passing skills. In July, Clark dished out 19 assists against the Dallas Wings. That set a record for the most assists in a WNBA game.

Later in July, the league shut down for a month so WNBA players could compete in the Olympics. That allowed Clark to take a break from basketball for the first time in 9 months. When the league started again in August, she went on a tear. The Fever won seven of their first eight games after the Olympic break. Those wins earned them a spot in the playoffs for the first time since 2016.

The Fever matched up with the Sun in the first round of the playoffs. Clark had come a long way since her first WNBA game. In two playoff games, Clark recorded 17 assists and only five turnovers. However, the Sun won both games to end Indiana's season.

CLARK'S COLLEGE CAREER

During her career at Iowa, Caitlin Clark increased her averages for points and assists per game every season. These are Clark's stats throughout the years.

2020–2021

26.6 points and **7.1 assists** per game

2021–2022

27.0 points and **8.0 assists** per game

2022–2023

27.8 points and **8.6 assists** per game

2023–2024

31.6 points and **8.9 assists** per game

The Indiana Fever beat the Chicago Sky 100–81 in August 2024. They played each other at the Wintrust Arena in Chicago, Illinois.

Despite the short playoff run, Clark's rookie season was a massive success. She easily won the Rookie of the Year Award. And she made the All-WNBA First Team, an honor for the five best players in the league. Clark was the first rookie to make that team since 2008.

Heading into the 2025 season, Indiana hired Stephanie White as their new head coach. She won Coach of the Year honors in 2023 while leading the Sun. The Fever also signed multiple **veterans** to improve their roster. The Fever was confident that with a better team, Clark could lift Indiana to a WNBA championship.

Clark stands alongside her Indiana Fever teammates.

GLOSSARY

assists (uh-SIHSTS) In basketball, assists are passes that lead to teammates making a point. Clark dished out 12 assists to help Iowa win.

draft (DRAFT) A draft is the process of teams picking new players, usually out of college. Clark was the first pick in the 2024 WNBA Draft.

layup (LAY-up) A layup is a shot in basketball taken from underneath the basket, worth two points. Clark scored a layup, sending the Big Ten Championship game to overtime.

overtime (OH-ver-tyme) Overtime is an extra period of play at the end of a tied sports contest to decide a winner. Iowa beat Nebraska in overtime at the 2024 Big Ten Tournament.

recruited (rih-KROO-ted) College coaches have recruited talented high-school athletes when they try to convince the athletes to play for their school. Iowa and Notre Dame recruited Clark.

rookie (RU-kee) A rookie describes someone who is a professional athlete in their first year in a league. Clark had a great rookie season in the WNBA.

triple-double (TRIH-pull DUH-bull) A triple-double is when a player reaches ten or more of three different statistics in one game. Clark recorded a triple-double in the 2023 Big Ten Tournament championship game.

upset (UP-set) An upset in sports is when a team wins a game they were expected to lose. Iowa upset South Carolina in the 2023 Final Four.

varsity (VAR-sih-tee) A varsity team is the top team at a high school. Clark played on Dowling Catholic's varsity basketball team for four years.

veterans (VEH-ter-unz) In sports, veterans are players who have played in a sports league for a long time. The Indiana Fever signed multiple veterans before the 2025 season.

FAST FACTS

- Caitlin Clark was born on January 22, 2002, in Des Moines, Iowa.
- During Clark's senior year in high school, she committed to the University of Iowa. She wanted to play college basketball close to home.
- As a junior in college, Clark led the Hawkeyes to their first national championship game.
- Clark finished her college career with 3,951 points, making her the leading scorer in college basketball history.
- Clark traveled to New York City for the WNBA Draft. Millions of fans tuned in to see the Indiana Fever select Clark with the top pick.
- In July 2024, Clark dished out 19 assists against the Dallas Wings. That set a record for the most assists in a WNBA game.
- Clark won WNBA Rookie of the Year in 2024 and lifted the Indiana Fever to the playoffs for the first time in 8 years.

ONE STRIDE FURTHER

- Clark played multiple sports growing up. Do you play any sports? If so, which one is your favorite?
- Clark played at Iowa to stay close to home. If you were making a similar choice, would you want to be close to your hometown or farther away? Why?
- After losing to Creighton in the 2022 NCAA Tournament, Clark worked hard to improve her basketball skills. How would you respond to a disappointing loss?

FIND OUT MORE

IN THE LIBRARY

Borzilleri, Meri-Jo. *Who Is Caitlin Clark?* New York, NY: Penguin Random House, 2025.

Buckley, James, Jr. *Talkin' Basketball.* Parker, CO: The Child's World, 2020.

Roggio, Sarah. *Caitlin Clark vs. Cheryl Miller: Who Would Win?* Minneapolis, MN: Lerner, 2026.

ON THE WEB

Visit our website for links about Caitlin Clark:

childsworld.com/links

Note to Parents, Caregivers, Teachers, and Librarians: We routinely verify our web links to make sure they are safe and active sites. So encourage your readers to check them out!

INDEX